THE WEDDING OF

AND

DATE

IMPORTANT NOTE:
For best results we recommend that you use a fountain pen, a marker or a felt tip to fill in this book. The pressure of a ball point pen will show through and spoil the following pages.

Other giftbooks by Exley:
My Wedding Planner   Marriage a Keepsake
Wedding Notebook   Happy Anniversary
A Bouquet of Wedding Jokes The Crazy World of Marriage

BORDER ILLUSTRATIONS BY JUDITH O'DWYER

Published simultaneously in 1995, 2004
by Exley Publications in Great Britain,
and Exley Giftbooks in the USA.
12

Edited by Helen Exley.
The moral right of the author has been asserted.
Copyright © Helen Exley 1995, 2004.

ISBN 978-1-86187-731-4

Pictures selected by Helen Exley.
Picture research by Image Select International.
Typeset by Delta, Watford.
Printed in China.

Helen Exley Giftbooks, 16 Chalk Hill, Watford,
Herts WD19 4BG, United Kingdom.
www.helenexleygiftbooks.com

IMPORTANT NOTE:
For best results we recommend that you
use a fountain pen, a marker or a felt tip
to fill in this book. The pressure of a ball
point pen will show through and spoil
the following pages.

Wedding

GUEST BOOK

A HELEN EXLEY GIFTBOOK

TO THE BRIDE & GROOM

FOR A GOOD LUCK MESSAGE, CONGRATULATIONS, A THANK-YOU FOR THE WEDDING CELEBRATIONS…

NAME

NAME

MESSAGE

MESSAGE

TO THE BRIDE & GROOM

HOPES FOR THEIR NEW LIFE TOGETHER, MESSAGES OF LOVE AND HAPPINESS, HEARTFELT CONGRATULATIONS…

NAME

MESSAGE

NAME

MESSAGE

TO THE BRIDE & GROOM

NAME

MESSAGE

NAME

MESSAGE

To the bride & groom

FOR HAPPY MEMORIES OF THE WEDDING DAY, GOOD WISHES FOR THE FUTURE, THOUGHTS OF LOVE AND CELEBRATION…

NAME

NAME

MESSAGE

MESSAGE

To THE BRIDE & GROOM

FOR A MESSAGE OF THANKS AND CONGRATULATIONS, YOUR HOPES FOR THE FUTURE, A COMMENT ON THE WEDDING DAY...

NAME

NAME

MESSAGE

MESSAGE

TO THE BRIDE & GROOM

NAME

NAME

MESSAGE

MESSAGE

TO THE BRIDE & GROOM

A TOAST TO THEIR FUTURE, YOUR MEMORIES OF THE WEDDING DAY, MESSAGES OF GOOD LUCK AND HAPPINESS...

NAME

NAME

MESSAGE

MESSAGE

TO THE BRIDE & GROOM

FOR A GOOD LUCK MESSAGE, CONGRATULATIONS, A THANK-YOU FOR THE WEDDING CELEBRATIONS…

NAME

NAME

MESSAGE

MESSAGE

TO THE BRIDE & GROOM

NAME

NAME

MESSAGE

MESSAGE

To the bride & groom

HOPES FOR THEIR NEW LIFE TOGETHER, MESSAGES OF LOVE AND HAPPINESS, HEARTFELT CONGRATULATIONS…

NAME | NAME

MESSAGE | MESSAGE

TO THE BRIDE & GROOM

FOR HAPPY MEMORIES OF THE WEDDING DAY, GOOD WISHES FOR THE FUTURE, THOUGHTS OF LOVE AND CELEBRATION…

NAME

NAME

MESSAGE

MESSAGE

TO THE BRIDE & GROOM

NAME

MESSAGE

NAME

MESSAGE

TO THE BRIDE & GROOM

FOR A MESSAGE OF THANKS AND CONGRATULATIONS, YOUR HOPES FOR THE FUTURE, A COMMENT ON THE WEDDING DAY...

NAME

NAME

MESSAGE

MESSAGE

TO THE BRIDE & GROOM

A TOAST TO THEIR FUTURE, YOUR MEMORIES OF THE WEDDING DAY, MESSAGES OF GOOD LUCK AND HAPPINESS...

NAME

NAME

MESSAGE

MESSAGE

To the bride & groom

NAME	NAME
MESSAGE	MESSAGE

To the bride & groom

FOR A GOOD LUCK MESSAGE, CONGRATULATIONS, A THANK-YOU FOR THE WEDDING CELEBRATIONS...

NAME

NAME

MESSAGE

MESSAGE

To the bride & groom

HOPES FOR THEIR NEW LIFE TOGETHER, MESSAGES OF LOVE AND HAPPINESS, HEARTFELT CONGRATULATIONS…

NAME

NAME

MESSAGE

MESSAGE

TO THE BRIDE & GROOM

NAME

MESSAGE

NAME

MESSAGE

TO THE BRIDE & GROOM

FOR HAPPY MEMORIES OF THE WEDDING DAY, GOOD WISHES FOR THE FUTURE, THOUGHTS OF LOVE AND CELEBRATION…

NAME

NAME

MESSAGE

MESSAGE

TO THE BRIDE & GROOM

FOR A MESSAGE OF THANKS AND CONGRATULATIONS, YOUR HOPES FOR THE FUTURE, A COMMENT ON THE WEDDING DAY…

NAME

NAME

MESSAGE

MESSAGE

TO THE BRIDE & GROOM

NAME

MESSAGE

NAME

MESSAGE

TO THE BRIDE & GROOM

A TOAST TO THEIR FUTURE, YOUR MEMORIES OF THE WEDDING DAY, MESSAGES OF GOOD LUCK AND HAPPINESS…

NAME

NAME

MESSAGE

MESSAGE

TO THE BRIDE & GROOM

FOR A GOOD LUCK MESSAGE, CONGRATULATIONS, A THANK-YOU FOR THE WEDDING CELEBRATIONS…

NAME

NAME

MESSAGE

MESSAGE

TO THE BRIDE & GROOM

NAME

MESSAGE

NAME

MESSAGE

To THE BRIDE & GROOM

HOPES FOR THEIR NEW LIFE TOGETHER, MESSAGES OF LOVE AND HAPPINESS, HEARTFELT CONGRATULATIONS…

NAME

NAME

MESSAGE

MESSAGE

TO THE BRIDE & GROOM

FOR HAPPY MEMORIES OF THE WEDDING DAY, GOOD WISHES FOR THE FUTURE, THOUGHTS OF LOVE AND CELEBRATION...

NAME

NAME

MESSAGE

MESSAGE

TO THE BRIDE & GROOM

NAME

NAME

MESSAGE

MESSAGE

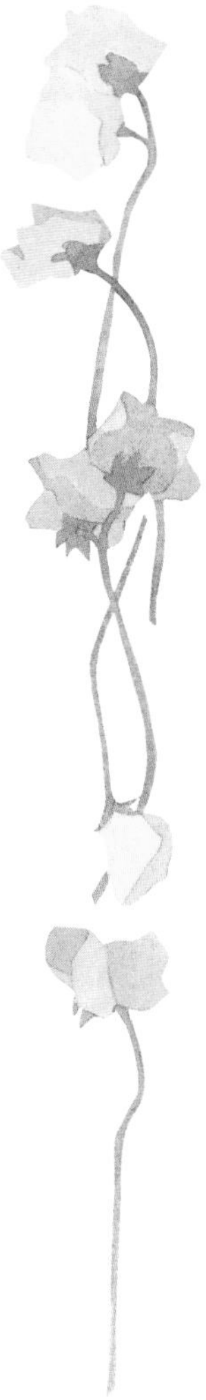

TO THE BRIDE & GROOM

FOR A MESSAGE OF THANKS AND CONGRATULATIONS, YOUR HOPES FOR THE FUTURE, A COMMENT ON THE WEDDING DAY...

NAME

NAME

MESSAGE

MESSAGE

TO THE BRIDE & GROOM

A TOAST TO THEIR FUTURE, YOUR MEMORIES OF THE WEDDING DAY, MESSAGES OF GOOD LUCK AND HAPPINESS…

NAME

NAME

MESSAGE

MESSAGE

To the Bride & Groom

NAME

MESSAGE

NAME

MESSAGE

TO THE BRIDE & GROOM

FOR A GOOD LUCK MESSAGE, CONGRATULATIONS, A THANK-YOU FOR THE WEDDING CELEBRATIONS…

NAME

NAME

MESSAGE

MESSAGE

TO THE BRIDE & GROOM

HOPES FOR THEIR NEW LIFE TOGETHER, MESSAGES OF LOVE AND HAPPINESS, HEARTFELT CONGRATULATIONS…

NAME

MESSAGE

NAME

MESSAGE

To THE BRIDE & GROOM

NAME

MESSAGE

NAME

MESSAGE

TO THE BRIDE & GROOM

FOR HAPPY MEMORIES OF THE WEDDING DAY, GOOD WISHES FOR THE FUTURE, THOUGHTS OF LOVE AND CELEBRATION…

NAME

NAME

MESSAGE

MESSAGE

TO THE BRIDE & GROOM

FOR A MESSAGE OF THANKS AND CONGRATULATIONS, YOUR HOPES FOR THE FUTURE, A COMMENT ON THE WEDDING DAY…

NAME

NAME

MESSAGE

MESSAGE

TO THE BRIDE & GROOM

NAME

MESSAGE

NAME

MESSAGE

TO THE BRIDE & GROOM

A TOAST TO THEIR FUTURE, YOUR MEMORIES OF THE WEDDING DAY, MESSAGES OF GOOD LUCK AND HAPPINESS...

NAME

NAME

MESSAGE

MESSAGE

TO THE BRIDE & GROOM

FOR A GOOD LUCK MESSAGE, CONGRATULATIONS, A THANK-YOU FOR THE WEDDING CELEBRATIONS…

NAME

NAME

MESSAGE

MESSAGE

TO THE BRIDE & GROOM

NAME

MESSAGE

NAME

MESSAGE

TO THE BRIDE & GROOM

HOPES FOR THEIR NEW LIFE TOGETHER, MESSAGES OF LOVE AND HAPPINESS, HEARTFELT CONGRATULATIONS...

NAME

NAME

MESSAGE

MESSAGE

TO THE BRIDE & GROOM

FOR HAPPY MEMORIES OF THE WEDDING DAY, GOOD WISHES FOR THE FUTURE, THOUGHTS OF LOVE AND CELEBRATION…

NAME

NAME

MESSAGE

MESSAGE

TO THE BRIDE & GROOM

NAME

NAME

MESSAGE

MESSAGE

TO THE BRIDE & GROOM

FOR A MESSAGE OF THANKS AND CONGRATULATIONS, YOUR HOPES FOR THE FUTURE, A COMMENT ON THE WEDDING DAY...

NAME

MESSAGE

NAME

MESSAGE

TO THE BRIDE & GROOM

A TOAST TO THEIR FUTURE, YOUR MEMORIES OF THE WEDDING DAY, MESSAGES OF GOOD LUCK AND HAPPINESS…

NAME

NAME

MESSAGE

MESSAGE

To the Bride & Groom

NAME

NAME

MESSAGE

MESSAGE

TO THE BRIDE & GROOM

FOR A GOOD LUCK MESSAGE, CONGRATULATIONS, A THANK-YOU FOR THE WEDDING CELEBRATIONS…

NAME

NAME

MESSAGE

MESSAGE

TO THE BRIDE & GROOM

NAME

MESSAGE

NAME

MESSAGE

TO THE BRIDE & GROOM

NAME

MESSAGE

NAME

MESSAGE

TO THE BRIDE & GROOM

FOR HAPPY MEMORIES OF THE WEDDING DAY, GOOD WISHES FOR THE FUTURE, THOUGHTS OF LOVE AND CELEBRATION…

NAME

NAME

MESSAGE

MESSAGE

TO THE BRIDE & GROOM

FOR A MESSAGE OF THANKS AND CONGRATULATIONS, YOUR HOPES FOR THE FUTURE, A COMMENT ON THE WEDDING DAY...

NAME

NAME

MESSAGE

MESSAGE

TO THE BRIDE & GROOM

NAME

NAME

MESSAGE

MESSAGE

TO THE BRIDE & GROOM

A TOAST TO THEIR FUTURE, YOUR MEMORIES OF THE WEDDING DAY, MESSAGES OF GOOD LUCK AND HAPPINESS…

NAME

NAME

MESSAGE

MESSAGE

TO THE BRIDE & GROOM

FOR A GOOD LUCK MESSAGE, CONGRATULATIONS, A THANK-YOU FOR THE WEDDING CELEBRATIONS…

NAME

MESSAGE

NAME

MESSAGE

TO THE BRIDE & GROOM

NAME

MESSAGE

NAME

MESSAGE

To the bride & groom

HOPES FOR THEIR NEW LIFE TOGETHER, MESSAGES OF LOVE AND HAPPINESS, HEARTFELT CONGRATULATIONS…

NAME

NAME

MESSAGE

MESSAGE

TO THE BRIDE & GROOM

FOR HAPPY MEMORIES OF THE WEDDING DAY, GOOD WISHES FOR THE FUTURE, THOUGHTS OF LOVE AND CELEBRATION…

NAME

NAME

MESSAGE

MESSAGE

TO THE BRIDE & GROOM

NAME

MESSAGE

NAME

MESSAGE

TO THE BRIDE & GROOM

FOR A MESSAGE OF THANKS AND CONGRATULATIONS, YOUR HOPES FOR THE FUTURE, A COMMENT ON THE WEDDING DAY...

NAME

NAME

MESSAGE

MESSAGE

TO THE BRIDE & GROOM

A TOAST TO THEIR FUTURE, YOUR MEMORIES OF THE WEDDING DAY, MESSAGES OF GOOD LUCK AND HAPPINESS...

NAME

NAME

MESSAGE

MESSAGE

TO THE BRIDE & GROOM

NAME

MESSAGE

NAME

MESSAGE

TO THE BRIDE & GROOM

FOR A GOOD LUCK MESSAGE, CONGRATULATIONS, A THANK-YOU FOR THE WEDDING CELEBRATIONS…

NAME

NAME

MESSAGE

MESSAGE

TO THE BRIDE & GROOM

HOPES FOR THEIR NEW LIFE TOGETHER, MESSAGES OF LOVE AND HAPPINESS, HEARTFELT CONGRATULATIONS…

NAME

NAME

MESSAGE

MESSAGE

TO THE BRIDE & GROOM

NAME

NAME

MESSAGE

MESSAGE

ACKNOWLEDGEMENTS

Exley Publications is very grateful to the following individuals and organizations for permission to reproduce their pictures. Whilst all reasonable efforts have been made to clear copyright and acknowledge sources and artists, Exley Publications would be happy to hear from any copyright holder who may have been omitted.

COVER: *Signing the Register*, Edmund Blair Leighton (1853-1922), City of Bristol Museum and Art Gallery, The Bridgeman Art Library.

PAGE 4: *Roses*, Jean Laudy (1877-1956), Whitford and Hughes, London, The Bridgeman Art Library.

PAGE 8: *The Wedding Morning*, Bacon, Lady Lever Art Gallery, Port Sunlight/Board of Trustees of the National Museums and Galleries on Merseyside.

PAGE 13: *Through the Room*, 1985, Ray Ellis A.W.S. (b. 1921), Chris Beetles Ltd., London, The Bridgeman Art Library.

PAGE 17: *Madonna Lilies in a Garden*, Walter Crane (1845-1915), Private Collection, The Bridgeman Art Library.

PAGE 21: *Die Toilette der Braut*, Gustave Courbet (1819-1877), Smith Coll. Museum, Northampton (Mass.), Archiv Fur Kunst.

PAGE 24: *The Wedding*, Walter Richard Sickert(1860-1942), Private Collection, The Bridgeman Art Library.

PAGE 28: *In the Dining Room*, Carl Helsoe (1863-1935), Private Collection, Edimedia, Paris.

PAGE 32: *Anemones*, © 1995 Diana Armfield, Private Collection, The Bridgeman Art Library.

PAGE 36: *An Elegant Soirée*, Victor Gabriel Gilbert (1847-1933), Fine Art Photographic Library Ltd.

PAGE 41: *The Wedding Feast*, Elek Gyori (1906-1958), Hungarian National Gallery, Budapest, The Bridgeman Art Library.

PAGE 44: *The Bride*, William Kennedy (1859-1918), Fine Art Photographic Library Ltd.

PAGE 49: *Signing the Register*, Edmund Blair Leighton (1853-1922), City of Bristol Museum and Art Gallery, The Bridgeman Art Library.

PAGE 53: *Snowcap Chrysanthemum*, Karen Armitage, Private Collection, The Bridgeman Art Library.

PAGE 57: *At the Breakfast Table*, Jan Theodore (1858-1928), Whitford and Hughes, London, The Bridgeman Art Library.

PAGE 60: *White Lilies*, Anders Zorn (1860-1920), Mora. (Dalarna), Zornmuseet.

PAGE 65: *Sylvia*, Sir Frank Dicksee (1853-1928), Sotheby's Transparency Library.

PAGE 69: *The Wedding Dress*, George Goodwin Kilburne (1839-1924), Phillips, the International Fine Art Auctioneers, The Bridgeman Art Library.

PAGE 72: *The Health of the Bride*, Stanhope Forbes (1857-1947), Tate Gallery, London/Art Resource.

PAGE 77: *Woman in Garden*, Claude Monet (1840-1926), Musée d'Orsay, Paris, Archiv fur Kunst.

PAGE 81: *Lady in a Pink Interior*, Patrick William Adam (1854-1929), Gavin Graham Gallery, London, The Bridgeman Art Library.

PAGE 84: *Agapanthus Molucela arrangement in a glass vase*, Karen Armitage, Private Collection, The Bridgeman Art Library.

PAGE 88: *A Herbaceous Border*, Hugh L. Norris (c. 1863-1942), Christopher Wood Gallery, London, The Bridgeman Art Library.

PAGE 92: *Pink Roses*, Princess Antonia du Portugal (1845-1913), Private Collection, Edimedia, Paris.